The Absolutely

MATH

dictionary

Every Kid's Guide to Mathematical Terms, Strategies, and Tables

Written by Theresa Fitzgerald

Illustrated by Stephanie O'Shaughnessy

Edited by Dianne Draze, Lisa Wood, and Sonsie Conroy

ISBN 1-59363-031-X

Prufrock Press Inc.
P.O. Box 8813
Waco, TX 76714-8813

For more information about Prufrock Press products, visit our website
http://www.prufrock.com

Contents

With many thanks to
Kristin Sonnemann-Grams,
Charlene Wendt
and
Rebecca McCormick

Dedicated with love to John and Amanda

Introduction

Every discipline has its own unique vocabulary, a group of words and definitions that people use to study or communicate information in this disciple. The key to understanding any subject is knowing the terminology. Likewise, mathematics has a vocabulary, not only words, but also symbols that allow people to have a common base of understanding. And like other disciplines, knowing the vocabulary of mathematics is having the power to unlock problems.

There are many keys to being a proficient math problem solver, and two of the most important elements to successful problem solving are:

- knowing what the problem is asking – understanding the vocabulary and being able to determine what strategy to employ
- knowing how to perform the operation(s) – being able to quickly and automatically perform the necessary operations.

This math dictionary provides information that will help math students in these two important areas of problem solving plus a wealth of other information, compiled in an easy-to-use format.

The Absolutely Essential Math Dictionary is much more than a compilation of words and definitions. This book has been organized to reflect the different areas of mathematics taught in elementary and junior high schools. Within each category are all the terms commonly used in this field of study, concise definitions, and many examples and illustrations. In addition, the last chapter provides instructions for basic operations and tables of commonly-used facts and equivalents.

This is a textbook that should be used throughout the year. It can be used on a daily basis in the whole-class setting to review the vocabulary and operations associated with whatever units of mathematics the class is studying. This daily review provides continuous reinforcement that leads to proficiency. The book can also be used on an individual basis. All a student needs to do is pull it out of his or her desk to have a quick reference to check what a term means or how an operation is performed. This cuts down on the chances of making mistakes, aids comprehension, and build self-reliance.

Once you use a reference like this book, you'll agree that it truly is absolutely essential. It will be the reference material you will use again and again to supplement and reinforce each topic in in your mathematics curriculum.

Numbers and Operations

Addends

Numbers in addition problems that are added together to find a sum.

Example:

3 + 7 = 10   **3** and **7** are **addends**

Addition

The process of uniting two or more numbers into a sum.

Arithmetic Progression

A series of numbers in which each number differs from the preceding number by a fixed amount. A series of numbers that follows a pattern.

Example:

1, 5, 9, 13, 17. . .

Ascending Order

Increasing from least to greatest, not necessarily according to a fixed pattern.

Example:

35, 37, 39, 41, 43, 45, 47, 49 is an ascending arithmetic progression

1, 5, 13, 40, 53 is a series of numbers in ascending order

Binary Numbers

A numerical system that is based on the number 2; each place has a value equal to a power of 2, as indicated or shown by the symbols 0 or 1.

Example:

base 10	1	2	3	4	5	6	7	8	9
base 2	1	10	11	100	101	110	111	1000	1001

Cardinal Numbers

Any number that is used for counting or answers the question "how many;" numbers such as 1, 2, 3, 47, 104.

Common Factor/Common Divisor

A factor that two or more numbers have in common. A number that divides 2 or more numbers without a remainder. The numerals that are the same when you build two different numbers with tiles.

Example:

(1,) (2,) 3, and 6 are the factors of 6

(1,) (2,) 4, and 8 are the factors of 8

The factors that 6 and 8 have in common, or share, are **1** and **2**.

Common Multiple

Any number that is a multiple of each of 2 or more numbers.

Example:

Multiples of 2	2	4	6	8	10	(12)	14	16	18 . . .
Multiples of 3	3	6	9	(12)	15	18	21	24	27 . . .
Multiples of 4	4	8	(12)	16	20	24	28	32	36 . . .
Multiples of 5	5	10	15	20	25	30	35	40	45 . . .
Multiples of 6	6	(12)	18	24	30	36	42	48	54 . . .

12 is a common multiple of 2, 3, 4 and 6.

Composite Number

A number that has factors other than one and itself. A number that can be built in more than one way using tiles. Composite numbers can be written as the product of prime numbers.

Example:

$6 = 2 \times 3$
$90 = 2 \times 5 \times 9$
$40 = 2 \times 2 \times 2 \times 5$

Counting Numbers

The positive whole numbers; the numbers 1, 2, 3, 4, 5, . . .
Also called natural numbers.

Descending Order

Decreasing from greatest to least, but not necessarily in a fixed pattern.

Example:

101, 90, 87, 72, 56, . . .

Difference

The answer to a subtraction problem.

Example:

7 - 5 = 2   **2** is the **difference** between the numbers

Dividend

The number in division that is to be divided.

Example:

$$\frac{5}{6)\overline{30}} \qquad \text{or} \qquad 30 \div 6 = 5 \qquad \textbf{30} \text{ is the } \textbf{dividend}$$

Divisibility Rules

2 - A number is divisible by two if it is even or if the last digit is divisible by 2.

3 - A number is divisible by 3 if the sum of its digits is divisible by 3.

4 - A number is divisible by 4 if the number formed by the last two digits are divisible by 4 or are two zeros.

5 - A number is divisible by 5 if the last digit is 5 or 0.

6 - A number is divisible by 6 if the number is even and is divisible by 3.

9 - A number is divisible by 9 if the sum of the digits is divisible by 9.

10 - A number is divisible by 10 if the last digit is a zero.

Divisible

Capable of being divided without a remainder.

Division

The process of division, meaning:

1) Breaking a number into smaller groups of equal quantities.

2) Repeated subtraction; subtracting the same number again and again.

Example:

$$4\overline{)12} = 3$$

4 is the **divisor**

12 is the **dividend**

3 is the **quotient**

Divisor

The number in a division problem by which the dividend is divided; the number used to divide by.

Example:

$$4\overline{)28} = 7 \qquad 28 \div 4 = 7$$

4 is the **divisor**

Equality

The property of being equal.
These things are true of equal numbers:

- $a = a$
- If $a = b$ then $b = a$
- If $a = b$ and $b = c$, then $a = c$

Even Number

Any number that is divisible by 2; a whole number that has 0, 2, 4, 6, or 8 in the ones place.

Expanded Form

Numbers broken up into their individual place values.

Example:

$$3{,}422 = 3{,}000 + 400 + 20 + 2$$
$$= (3 \times 1000) + (4 \times 100) + (2 \times 10) + 2$$
$$= (3 \times 10^3) + (4 \times 10^2) + (2 \times 10^1) + (2 \times 10^0)$$

Fact Family

There are usually four members to every fact family. Fact families use three numbers to make the combinations of addition and subtraction equations or multiplication and division equations that can be used with the three numbers chosen.

Addition/Subtraction (7, 3, 10)

$7 + 3 = 10$ $10 - 3 = 7$
$3 + 7 = 10$ $10 - 7 = 3$

Multiplication/Division (3, 8, 24)

$3 \times 8 = 24$ $24 \div 8 = 3$
$8 \times 3 = 24$ $24 \div 3 = 8$

Factor

The numbers that are multiplied together to get a product or answer.

Example:

$6 \times 7 = 42$ **6** and **7** are the **factors**

Factorial

The product of consecutive numbers, always starting with 1.
It is symbolized by **!**

Example:

$3! = 1 \times 2 \times 3 = 6$ $6! = 1 \times 2 \times 3 \times 4 \times 5 \times 6 = 720$

Greater Than/Less Than

A way of comparing two groups of objects using the symbols $>$ and $<$
The symbols for greater than, less than can be remembered in these ways:

Example:

Two are greater than one. The side with two ends points towards the larger number.	Mouths with sharp teeth like to take bigger bites!	
		$8 < 11$
		$12 > 3$

Greatest Common Factor

The largest number that is a common factor (divisor) of two numbers.

Example:

Factors of 30	1, 2, 3, 5, 6, 10, 15 30
Factors of 24	1, 2, 3, 4, 6, 8, 12, 24
Common factors	1, 2, 3, 6

Greatest common factor is **6**

Hindu-Arabic Numbers

A base-10, place-value number system that uses the symbols 0, 1, 2, 3, 4, 5, 6, 7, 8 and 9; also called Arabic numbers.

Infinite

Not able to be measured or counted. The symbol for infinity is ∞.
Infinite sets are noted with the symbol ..., which means that the numbers go on and on forever.

Example:

{2, 4, 6, 8, 10, 12, . . .}

Integer

Positive and negative whole numbers and zero; not fractions or mixed numbers or decimals.

Example:

- 3, -1, 0, 5, and 17 are integers.

$\frac{1}{2}$, $3\frac{1}{4}$ and .34 are not integers.

Inverse Operations

The opposite operation. Subtraction is the inverse of addition. Division is the inverse of multiplication.

Irrational Numbers

Numbers that cannot be written as the ratio of two integers.

π, $\sqrt{7}$, $\sqrt[3]{11}$ are irrational.

Laws of Arithmetic

There are several laws that govern basic arithmetic operations. They are:

- **Commutative Law (Order Property)**
  Changing the order of the addends or factors does not change the sum or the product.

  Addition   Multiplication
  $a + b = b + a$ $a \times b = b \times a$

- **Associative Law (Grouping Property)**
  Changing the way the addends or factors are grouped does not change the sum or the product.

  Addition   Multiplication
  $(a + b) + c = a + (b + c)$ $(a \times b) \times c = a \times (b \times c)$

- **Distributive Law**
  A number that is multiplied times the sum of two or more numbers is the same as the sum of that number multiplied by each of the numbers separately.

  $a \times (b + c) = (a \times b) + (a \times c)$

Less Than

See Greater than/Less than

Lowest Common Multiple (LCM)

The lowest multiple that two or more numbers have in common.

Example:

Multiples of 2 - 2, 4, 6, 8, 10, 12, 14, 16, 18, 20, 24, 26

Multiples of 3 - 3, 6, 8, 9, 12, 15, 18, 21, 24, 27, 30, 33

6, 12, 18, and 24 are all multiples of 2 and 3, but 6 is the lowest common multiple because it is the first number that is in both sets.

Minuend

A number from which another number is subtracted.

$$\begin{array}{r} 23 \\ -5 \\ \hline 18 \end{array}$$

23 is the **minuend**

Multiple

A number that is the product of a certain number and another whole number.

Examples:

2 x 6 = 12   **12** is a **multiple** of 2 and of 6

multiples of 6 are 6, 12, 18, 24, 30 . . .
multiples of 2 are 2, 4, 6, 8, 10, 12, 14 . . .

Multiplication

Repeated addition. Adding the same number a given number of times.

Example:

4 x 3 = 12 is the same as 3 + 3 + 3 + 3 = 12

Numbers, Sets of

Natural or counting numbers - {1, 2, 3, 4, 5, 6, …}
Whole numbers - {0, 1, 2, 3, 4, 5, 6, …}
Integers - { … , -4, -3, -2, -1, 0, 1, 2, 3, 4, …}
Rational numbers - the set of integers plus numbers that can be
          written as proper and improper fractions.
Irrational numbers - the set of numbers that are not rational

Numerals

Symbols used to denote numbers.
3 is a numeral that stands for three things (❤❤❤)

Odd Number

A whole number which, when divided by 2, has a remainder of 1; a whole number that has a 1, 3, 5, 7, or 9 in the ones place.

Ordinal Numbers

A numeral that expresses degree, quality or position; numerals that show order.
Ordinal - first, second, third
Cardinal - 1, 2, 3

Pair

A set of two; two of a kind

✳✳ = 1 pair	✳✳ ✳✳ = 3 pairs ✳✳	✳✳ = 3 pairs ✳✳ with one ✳✳ left over ✳

Place Value

The value given to the space a digit holds because of its place in the numeral.

Example:

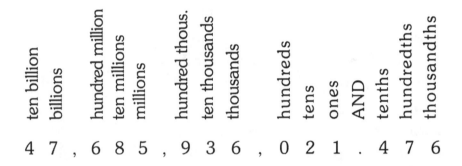

Prime Factors

The prime numbers which when multiplied will result in the given numeral.

Example:

Breaking a number down to its primes (primes are circled)

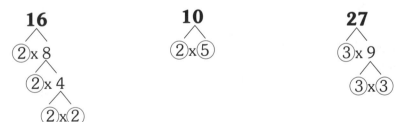

prime factors are   prime factors are   prime factors are

1, 2, 2, 2, 2   1, 2, 5   1, 3, 3, 3

Prime Number

A whole number greater than one that only has itself and the number one as factors; a number that can be built only one way using tiles.

Example:

17 is a prime number because:

- it can only be built using 1 row of 17 tiles
- 1 x 17 = 17
- its only factors are the numbers 1 and 17

The first ten prime numbers are 2, 3, 5, 7, 11, 13, 17, 19, 23, 29

Product

The answer to a multiplication problem.

Example:

4 x 8 = 32 ⟵⟶ **32** is the **product**

Progression

A sequence of numbers that has a fixed pattern.

- **Arithmetic progression** - Each term is a result of adding or subtracting a given number.
  Example: 3, 7, 11, 15, 19, . . .

- **Geometric progression** - Each term is obtained by multiplying the preceding term by a given number.
  Example: 1, 3, 9, 27, 81, . . .

Quotient

The number that is the answer to a division problem, not including the remainder.

Example:

$$
\begin{array}{r}
7 \\
6\overline{)42} \\
-42 \\
\hline
0
\end{array}
$$

42 ÷ 7 = 6   **7** is the **quotient**

Rational Numbers

A number that can be expressed as a fraction; includes integers ($\frac{3}{1}$, $\frac{23}{1}$), fractions ($\frac{1}{4}$, $\frac{1}{100}$), and terminating or repeating decimals (.25, .333...).

Relationship Symbols

Symbols used to compare the values of two or more numbers or expressions. The most common are $=$, $\neq$, $>$, and $<$.

Remainder

The number smaller than the divisor that is left over after the division process has been completed. What's left over after you have put all that you can into equal groups.

Example:

$10 \div 3 = 3\,r\,1$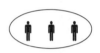

Roman Numerals

Roman letters used to represent numbers. These are usually written in capitals. If there is a bar, or line, over the letter(s) that means that number is multiplied by 1,000.

1 = I	9 = IX	17 = XVII
2 = II	10 = X	18 = XVIII
3 = III	11 = XI	19 = XIX
4 = IV	12 = XII	20 = XX
5 = V	13 = XIII	50 = L
6 = VI	14 = XIV	100 = C
7 = VII	15 = XV	500 = D
8 = VIII	16 = XVI	1,000 = M

Sequence

A grouping of numbers that are arranged so there is a pattern; usually written with the numbers separated by commas (2, 7, 4, 9, 6, 11, 8, ...)

Square

To multiply a number by itself. $4^2 = 4 \times 4$ or 16

Square Number

A number that is the square of another number or can be represented by a square array of dots or tiles.

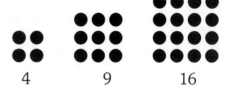

4   9   16

Square Root

A number which when multiplied by itself will produce a given number.

Example:

The square root of 49 is written $\sqrt{49} = +7$ or -7

The principal square root is the positive square root; $\sqrt{100} = 10$

Subtraction

The operation of finding the difference between two numbers.

Subtrahend

The number that is subtracted.

$9 - 6 = 3$ **6** is the **subtrahend**

Sum

The answer to an addition problem.

Example:

In the problem $4 + 5 = 9$, 9 is the sum

Whole Number

A positive number without a fraction or decimal part; $\{0, 1, 2, 3, \ldots, 10, 11, 12, \ldots\}$

Example:

1, 34, and 256 are whole numbers.

$\frac{3}{4}$, $5\frac{2}{3}$, .45, and 3.5 are not whole numbers.

Zero

The numeral indicating none.

Measurement

Area

The measurement surface of a region in square units. To find the area, count the squares you could fit inside the object, or multiply the length times the width.

3 units

2 units

Area = 6 square units

Capacity

The volume of a space figure or the amount of space an object has to fill. How much liquid something will hold.

Cubic

Having three dimensions; a cubic solid will have length, width, and height, like a block. Cubic measurements are shown with a small 3 above and to the right the unit measurement (M3).

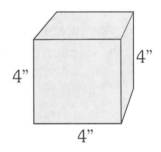

4"

4"

4"

Volume = 4 x 4 x 4 = 64 in ^{3}

Degree

A unit of measure for angles. ⟶
A circle is divided into 360 degrees.

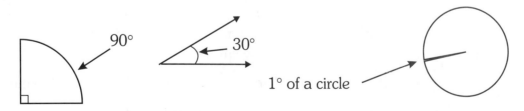

90°

30°

1° of a circle

Dimension

Measurement in length, width, depth, or height; the size of something.

Distance

The length of a straight line segment; how far it is from one point to another.

Estimate

To find an answer that is close to the exact answer. Your best guess.

Length

One-dimension measure; the distance from one end to the other end of a line segment; how long something is.

Measurement

The size or dimensions of something determined by measuring.

Metric Measurement

- **Capacity (volume)**

milliliter (mL)	1000 milliliters = 1 liter
liter (L)	1 liter = 1,000 milliliters
kiloliter (kL)	1 kiloliter = 1,000 liters

- **Length**

millimeter (mm)	*about as thick as the skinny part of a dime* 10 millimeter = 1 centimeter
centimeter (cm)	*about as wide as your little finger is across* 10 centimeter = 1 decimeter 100 centimeter = 1 meter
decimeter (dm)	1 decimeter = 10 centimeter 10 decimeter = 1 meter
meter (m)	1 meter = 10 dm = 100 cm = 1,000 mm
kilometer (km)	*used to measure long distances* 1 kilometer = 1,000 meters

Metric Measurement, continued

- **Weight**

milligram (mg)	1,000 milligram = 1 gram
gram (g)	*about the mass of a paper clip* 1 gram = 1,000 milligrams 1,000 grams = 1 kilogram
kilogram (kg)	1,000 grams = 1 kilogram

Perimeter

The distance around a figure. To find the perimeter, find the measurement of each side of the object and then add them up.

3 units

2 units

$$p = 3 + 2 + 3 + 2 = 10 \text{ units}$$

Protractor

An instrument divided into degrees, used for measuring angles.

Rounding

Expressing a number as the nearest multiple of 10 (10, 100, 1000...). If the number to the right of the place you are rounding to is 0-4, the number stays the same. If it is 5-9, the number rounds to the next greater number.

Example:

Rounding to the 10s place
566 → 570
562 → 560

Rounding to the 100s place
566 → 600
536 → 500

Ruler

A tool used for measuring and for drawing straight lines, usually divided into units and fractional parts of the units, such as inches or centimeters.

Scale

Any instrument that is divided into equal units and can be used to measure. Rulers, thermometers, and weighing devices are examples of scales.

Standard Measurements

- **Capacity**

cup (c.)	4 cups = 1 quart
pint (pt.)	2 pints = 1 quart
quart (qt.)	4 quarts = 1 gallon
gallon (gal.)	1 gallon = 4 quarts

- **Length**

inch (in. or ")	12 inches = 1 foot
foot (ft. or ')	1 foot = 12 inches
yard (yd.)	1 yard = 3 feet = 36 inches
mile (mi.)	1 mile = 5,280 feet

- **Weight**

ounce (oz.)	16 ounces = 1 pound
pound (lb.)	1 pound = 16 ounces
ton	1 ton = 2,000 pounds

Surface Area

The combined areas of all surfaces of a three-dimensional figure.

Example:

The surface area of a cube with sides equal to 3 is
$6 \times 3^2 = 6 \times 9 = 54$
area of one face = $3 \times 3 = 9$
There are 6 faces, so $9 \times 6 = 54$

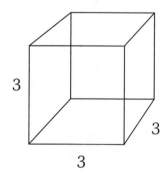

Temperature

The measure of warmth or coldness of an object.

- **Celsius** - Metric or centigrade scale of measurement of temperature.

  $0°$ C = freezing point of water

  $100°$ C = boiling point of water

  $20°$ C = normal room temperature

- **Fahrenheit** - Standard scale of measurement of temperature.

  $32°$ F = freezing point of water

  $212°$ F = boiling point of water

  $70°$ F = normal room temperature

Thermometer

An instrument used for measuring temperatures in Celsius, Fahrenheit, or both.

Time

a.m.   The time from 12:00 midnight to noon.

p.m.   The time from 12:00 noon to midnight.

60 seconds = 1 minute	365 or 366 days = 1 year
60 minutes = 1 hour	10 years = 1 decade
24 hours = 1 day	100 years = 1 century
7 days = 1 week	1,000 years = 1 millennium

Unit

A standard of measurement such as inches, feet, yards, miles, millimeters, centimeters, meters, grams, ounces, or pounds. Any amount used as a standard for measuring area, length, or volume.

Volume

The amount of space, measured in cubic units something takes up.

volume 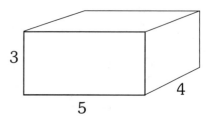 = length x width x height (V = L x W x H)

$$v = 3 \times 4 \times 5 = 60$$

volume = $\pi\, r^2\, h$

volume = $\dfrac{1}{3}\, \pi\, r^2\, h$

Weight

The gravitational pull on an object. The heaviness of an object; how much something weighs. Common units of measurement are ounce, pound, gram, kilogram, and ton.

Width

The distance from one side of an object to the other side; how wide something is.

Algebra

Absolute Value

The value of a number regardless of its sign; denoted by the numeral between two parallel lines, like $|+5|$. This is distance from the origin to that number on a number line.

Example:

$|+3| = 3$ and $|-3| = 3$

Binomial

A math expression that has two terms

Example:

5 + 11   2x + 4   3x + 2y

Coefficient

The numerical part of an algebraic term.

Example:

$3x^2$	3 is the coefficient
2y	2 is the coefficient
5(a + b)	5 is the coefficient

Equation

A number sentence that uses the equal sign. Everything on one side of an equal sign (=) has to equal everything on the other side.

Examples:

8 + 4 = 12	4 x 5 = 20	7 − 3 = 4
9 ÷ 3 = 3	35 - 23 = 10 + 2	7 + 4 + 3 = 2 x 7

Exponent

A small symbol placed above and to the right of another symbol that shows how many times the base is to be multiplied by itself.

Example:

$$b^3 = b \times b \times b$$
$$5^4 = 5 \times 5 \times 5 \times 5$$
$$7^2 = 7 \times 7$$

Formula

A set of symbols that expresses a mathematical fact or rule.

Examples:

area □	$a = l \times w$	perimeter □	$p = 2l + 2w$
area ○	$a = \pi r^2$	circumference ○	$c = \pi d$

Identity Element

A number that does not change the value when a certain operation is performed.

- **Addition and Subtraction** - 0 is the identity element.
  $$0 + 3 = 3 \text{ and } 3 - 0 = 3$$

- **Multiplication and Division** - 1 is the identity element.
  $$1 \times 5 = 5 \text{ and } 5 \div 1 = 5$$

Inequality

Not equal. A statement in which one expression is greater than (>), less than (<) or not equal (≠) to another.

Negative Number

A number less than zero. These numbers are written with a negative sign in front of them, like -5, -26 or -100.

negative integers

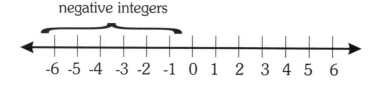

26

Number Sentence

A statement that involves numbers and their relationship or equality. Number sentences can be true, false or open.

Example:

$5 \times 9 = 45$	true
$9 + 11 = 4$	false
$6 + \square = 17$	open

Pascal's Triangle

An array of numbers, made popular by Blaise Pascal. One use of the triangle is finding the binomial coefficients for expressions like $(x + y)^z$.

```
                        1
                    1       1
                1       2       1
            1       3       3       1
        1       4       6       4       1
    1       5      10      10       5       1
1       6      15      20      15       6       1
```

Positive Number

A number greater than zero. On the number line these numbers are to the right of zero.

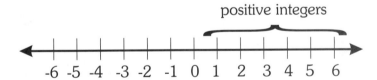

Power

The result of the repeated multiplication of a number by itself.

Example:

$3^2 = 3 \times 3 = 9$	9 is the second power of 3.
$2^4 = 2 \times 2 \times 2 \times 2 = 16$	16 is the fourth power of 2.

Properties

- **Associative (grouping) property** - Changing the grouping of the numbers does not change the sum or product.

$$(2 \times 3) \times 4 = 2 \times (3 \times 4) \qquad (6 + 1) + 3 = 6 + (1 + 3)$$
$$6 \times 4 = 2 \times 12 \qquad\qquad 7 + 3 = 6 + 4$$
$$24 = 24 \qquad\qquad\qquad 10 = 10$$

- **Commutative (order) property** - Changing the order of the addends or factors does not change the sum or the product. If you change the order of the addends or factors, the sum or product still stays the same.

$$5 + 12 = 12 + 5 \qquad\qquad 7 \times 9 = 9 \times 7$$

- **Distributive property** - The product of a number and the sum of two numbers is the same as the sum of the products of the number times each of the other numbers.

$$3\,(4 + 5) = 3 \times 4 + 3 \times 5$$
$$3 \times 9 \quad = \quad 12 + 15$$
$$27 \quad = \quad 27$$

- **Zero property**

Addition - the sum of a number and zero is that number.

$$6 + 0 = 6 \qquad 113 + 0 = 113$$

Multiplication - The product of a number and zero is zero.

$$7 \times 0 = 0 \qquad 248 \times 0 = 0$$

- **One property**

Multiplication - The product of a number and one is that number.

$$7 \times 1 = 7 \qquad 58 \times 1 = 58$$

Division - The quotient of a number divided by one is that number.

$$8 \div 1 = 8 \qquad 27 \div 1 = 27$$

Square

To multiply a number by itself; to raise a number to the second power.

$4^2 = 4 \times 4 = 16$

Square Root

The number which then multiplied by itself will produce a given number. The symbol for square root is $\sqrt{}$.

$$\sqrt{49} = 7 \qquad\qquad \sqrt{144} = 12$$

Subset

A set that is part of another set. The symbol is $\subset$.

{1, 3, 5, 7} is a subset of {1, 2, 3, 4, 5, 6, 7, 8}
{1, 3, 5, 7} $\subset$ {1, 2, 3, 4, 5, 6, 7, 8}

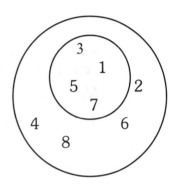

Symbol

A letter or mark that stands for a quantity, operation or relationship. Some symbols are 5, x, ÷, <, $\sqrt{}$ and =.

Unknown

The symbol in an equation for which you must find a solution that will make the equation true.

$3y - 4 = 10$ \qquad y is the unknown

Variable

A quantity that can have several different values; anything that changes.

Geometry

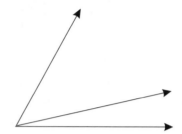

Adjacent Angles

Two angles that have a common vertex and one common side.

Altitude

See Height.

Angle

The figure made by two rays meeting at a point (a vertex). We measure the difference between the two lines in degrees.

- **Acute Angle**
  An angle with a measure less than 90°.

- **Right Angle**
  An angle that has the same shape as the corner of a square. A 90° angle.

- **Obtuse Angle**
  An angle whose measure is greater than 90°.

- **Straight Angle**
  An angle that measures 180°.

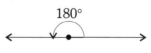

Arc

A segment of a circle.

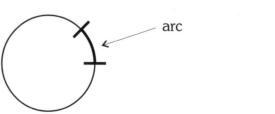

Axis

A line that is used to form a graph. The x-axis (abscissa) is the horizontal axis, and the y-axis (ordinate) is the vertical axis.

Base

The line segment that is the foundation of a geometric figure.

Bisect

To divide into two equal parts.

Center

A point equally distant from all points on the circumference of a circle or surface of a sphere.

Chord

A line that connects two points on a circle.

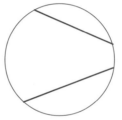

Circle

A closed curve in which all of the points are the same distance from the point in the center. The distance from the center of the circle to any point on the circle is the radius.

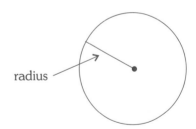

Circumference

The outer boundary or perimeter of a circle or circular surface; the distance around the outside of a circle.

C = 2 x 3.14 x radius   © = 2·π· r)

C = 3.14 x diameter   © = π· d)

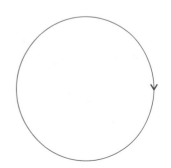

Collinear

Lying on the same straight line.
In the drawing below, points A, B and C are collinear.

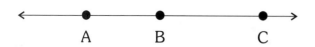

Complementary Angles

Two angles that together equal 90°

∠ABC and ∠CBD are complementary.

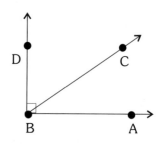

Cone

A solid figure that has a circular bottom
and one flat face.

Congruent

Figures that have the same size and shape.
The symbol for congruency is ≅.

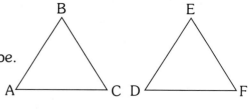

△ ABC ≅ △ DEF

Coordinates

The two numbers in a number
pair, used to find or define the
position of a point on a plane
or a grid. Also called a
number pair and an ordered
pair.

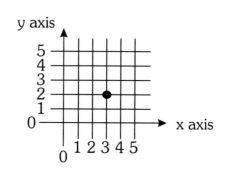

Example:

The illustration shows the point (3, 2)

Corresponding Parts

Parts, such as points, sides or angles, of two congruent figures that have the same position and are the same size.

Example:

Side AC corresponds to DF and angle A corresponds to angle D.

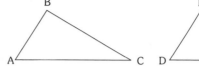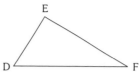

Cube

A three-dimensional figure that has six square faces. A cube has six faces, eight vertices and twelve edges.

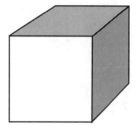

Cylinder

A three-dimensional figure that has two circular faces.

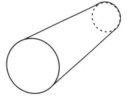

Decagon

A polygon with ten sides and ten angles; also called a 10-gon.

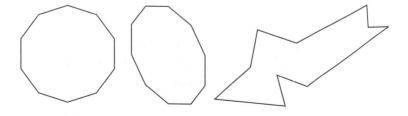

Diagonal

A line extending in a slanting manner from corner to corner in a polygon.

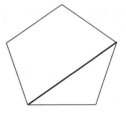

Diameter

A special kind of chord that passes through the center of a circle joining two opposite points on the circle; the length of a diameter is equal to two radii; it divides a circle into two equal parts called semicircles.

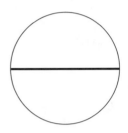

Dimension

The number of basic units used to measure a geometric figure.

- **one-dimensional**

- **two-dimensional**

- **three-dimensional**

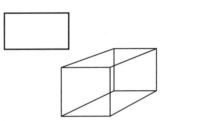

Dodecagon

A polygon with twelve sides and twelve angles; also called a 12-gon.

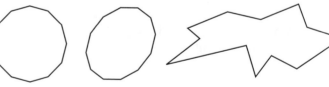

Edge

A straight line segment that is the intersection of two faces of a solid figure; the place where two faces meet.

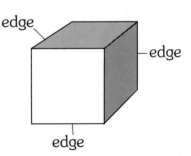

edge

edge

edge

Ellipse

An oval. A closed plane curve that has two centers (foci) that define the shape and size of the outer perimeter.

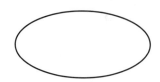

Equiangular

Having all angles equal. A square is equiangular.

Equilateral

Having all the sides equal.

Exterior Angles

An angle on the outside of a polygon that is formed by the extension of one side and the adjacent side of the polygon.

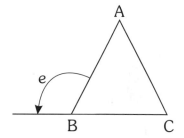

Face

One of the plane figures that make up a space figure.

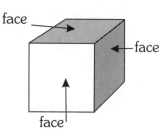

Height

The vertical distance from the base to the highest point. Also called altitude. In a triangle the height is the perpendicular distance from the vertex to the opposite side.

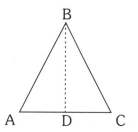

Hemisphere

Half a sphere.

Heptagon

A polygon with seven sides and seven angles; also called a 7-gon.

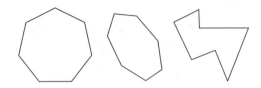

Hexagon

A polygon with six sides and six angles; also called a 6-gon.

Horizontal

Parallel to the horizon; perpendicular to the vertical.

Hypotenuse

The side of a right triangle that is opposite the right angle.

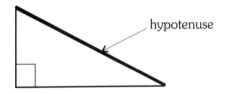

hypotenuse

Icosagon

A polygon with twenty sides and twenty angles; also called a 20-gon.

Image

The visual picture or likeness of something produced by the reflection from a mirror.

Interior Angle

An angle on the inside of a polygon that is formed by two adjacent sides of the polygon.

Intersecting Lines

Lines that meet at a point.

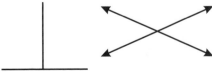

Irregular Polygon

A polygon in which the sides are not the same length and not all angles have the same measure.

Line

A one-dimensional straight path that is endless in both directions.

Line Segment

A portion (or part) of a straight line. There is a point at each end of a line segment and sometimes the ends will be labeled.

Midpoint

A point that is equal distance from the two end points of a line segment.

midpoint

Nonagon

A polygon with nine sides and nine angles; also called a 9-gon.

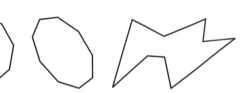

Number Pair

The numbers that are used to give the location of a point on a graph. *See Coordinates.*

Octagon

A polygon with eight sides and eight angles; also called an 8-gon.

Origin

In a coordinate system or graph, the point where the axes intersect; the base point. The starting point of a graph.

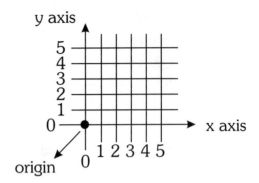

Parallel Lines

Lines that do not intersect and would not ever cross if they were extended. Lines that are equidistance at all points.

Parallelogram

A quadrilateral that has two pairs of opposite sides that are equal and parallel. In a parallelogram, opposite angles are equal and adjacent angles are supplementary.

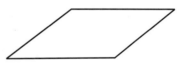

Pentagon

A polygon with five sides and five angles; also called a 5-gon.

Perimeter

The distance around; the sum of the sides of a geometric figure.

Example:

    perimeter = a + b + c + d

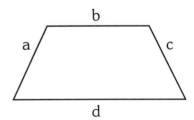

Perpendicular Lines

A special kind of intersecting lines. These are
lines that intersect to form a right (90°) angle.

Pi

The ratio between the circumference and diameter of a circle ($\pi = \frac{C}{d}$).

It is denoted with the symbol π. It is approximately 3.14159265...
(often shortened to the hundredths place to 3.14).

Plane Figure

A two dimensional shape. Figures that lie on a flat surface.

Examples:

regular shapes   **regular polygons**   **irregular polygons**

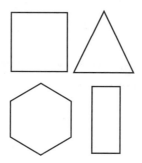

Polygon

A closed figure that is formed entirely by line
segments. Examples include pentagon, hexagon,
heptagon, octagon, trapezoid, and square.

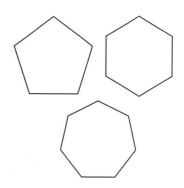

- **Regular Polygon**
  All the sides of the figure are the
  same length and all angles have
  the same measure.

Polyhedron

A three-dimensional figure with many faces; includes cubes, pyramids and
prisms.

Prism

A solid figure whose ends are parallel, congruent (equal size and shape) polygons and whose sides are parallelograms.

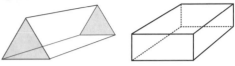

Pyramid

A geometric solid formed by triangles. The faces on a pyramid are triangles that meet at a point (vertex). They can have different shaped bases and are named by the shapes of their bases.

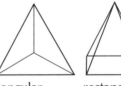

triangular pyramid   rectangular pyramid   square pyramid

Pythagorean Theorem

A theorem that states that in a right triangle the sum of the squares of the two sides is equal to the square of the hypotenuse.
$a^2 + b^2 = c^2$

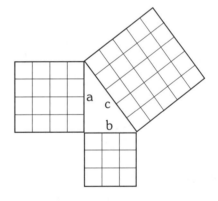

Quadrant

A quarter of a plane has been divided by perpendicular lines. Circles can be divided into quadrants. In coordinate geometry, the plane is divided into four quadrants by the x-axis and the y-axis.

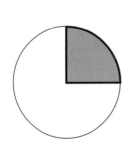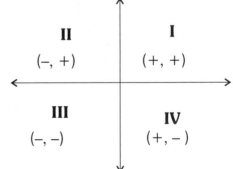

Quadrilateral

Any polygon with four sides. Examples include square, rectangle, parallelogram, rhomboid, rhombus, trapezoid, and trapezium.

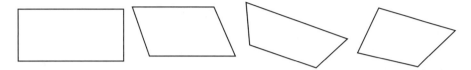

Radius

A straight line that extends from the center of a circle to a point on the circumference of a circle. The radius equals one half of the diameter.

Ray

A straight line that extends from a point forever in one direction.

Rectangle

A quadrilateral and parallelogram that has four right angles and two pairs of opposite sides that are the same length.

Rectangular Prism

A space figure that has rectangles and squares for faces. Rectangular prisms are in the shape of a box, and they have 6 faces, 8 vertices and 12 edges.

Reflection

The image of an object as seen in a mirror.

Rhomboid

A quadrilateral and parallelogram in which opposite sides are parallel, but there are no right angles.

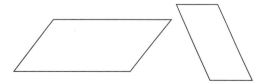

Rhombus

A quadrilateral and parallelogram that has four equal sides, but no right angles.

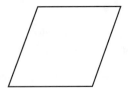

Rotation

To turn around a center point.

Segment

A piece or portion of something, such as a line.

Semicircle

Half a circle.

Similar

Figures that have the same shape, but not the same size.

Slope

The amount of slant or inclination of a line on a coordinate graph.

$$\text{slope} = \frac{\text{change in y}}{\text{change in x}}$$

Space Figure

Another way to describe a solid shape. Space figures have volume, meaning they take up space. They are not flat but are three dimensional.

Sphere

A space figure in which every point is equidistant (same distance) from the center; shaped like a ball.

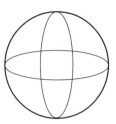

Square

A quadrilateral and parallelogram that has four equal sides and four equal 90° angles. A square is a special type of rectangle.

Supplementary Angles

Two angles whose sum is 180°.

Example:

$\angle ABC + \angle CBD = 180°$

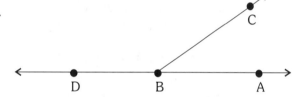

Surface Area

The sum of the areas of all the flat surfaces of a three-dimensional figure.

Symmetrical

The characteristics of a figure that can be folded in half and the two halves will be identical.

• **Horizontal Symmetry**
Parallel to the horizon.

• **Vertical Symmetry**
Perpendicular to the horizon.

Transversal

A straight line that intersects a
set of lines.

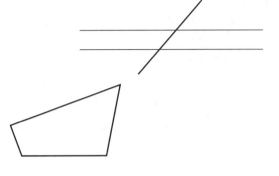

Trapezium

A quadrilateral in which no two
sides are parallel.

Trapezoid

A quadrilateral that has exactly one
pair of parallel sides.

Triangle

A plane figure with three sides and three angles.
The sum of a triangle's angles equals 180°.

- **Equilateral Triangle**
  A triangle in which all three sides are the
  same length and all three angles are 60°.

- **Isosceles Triangle**
  A triangle that has two sides the
  same length.

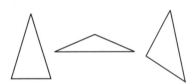

- **Right Triangle**
  A triangle that has a right (90°) angle.

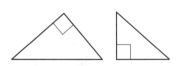

- **Scalene Triangle**
  A triangle in which no sides are
  the same length.

Triangular Prism

A solid figure that has two triangular faces and three rectangular faces, six vertices and nine edges.

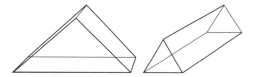

Vertex (vertices)

The point of intersection of rays or line segments; corners. In plane figures, the point opposite the base.

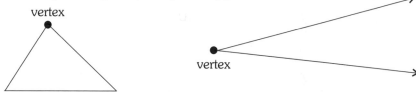

Vertical

Perpendicular to the horizon; upright.

Vertically Opposite Angles

Angles with a common vertex whose sides are extensions of the other angle's sides. Vertical angles are equal.

∠A and ∠C are vertically opposite.
∠B and ∠D are vertically opposite.

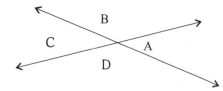

Fractions, Decimals, Ratio and Percent

Decimal

A special kind of fraction that has a power of 10 (10, 100, 1,000…) for a denominator. Decimals are part of a whole. They are written with a decimal point, using place value, instead of as a fraction.

$$\frac{47}{100} = .47$$

$$3\frac{2}{10} = 3.2$$

(place value chart: and • ___ ___ ___ , labeled tenths, hundredths, thousandths)

Decimal Fractions

A fraction whose denominator is a power of 10 (10, 100, 1000…).

Example

$$\frac{2}{10} = .2 \qquad \frac{34}{100} = .34 \qquad \frac{56}{1000} = .056$$

Decimal Point

A dot written in a number that separates the whole number from the fractional part. The decimal point is read as "and."

Denominator

The number below the line in a fraction. It shows how many equal pieces the whole has been divided into.

Example:

$$\frac{6}{8}$$ 8 is the **denominator**

- **Common Denominator**
  A common multiple of the denominators of two or more fractions.

  Example:

  $\frac{1}{2}$ multiples of 2 - 2, 4, 6, 8, (10,) 12, 14, 16, 18, (20,) 22, . . .

  $\frac{3}{5}$ multiples of 5 - 5, (10,) 15, (20,) 25, 30, 35, 40, 45, 50, . . .

  10 and 20 are multiples of 2 and 5, so 10 and 20 are common multiples of $\frac{1}{2}$ and $\frac{3}{5}$.

- **Lowest Common Denominator (LCD)**
  The lowest denominator that two or more fractions have in common.

  Example:

  $\frac{1}{2}$ multiples of 2 - 2, 4, (6,) 8, 10, 12, 14, 16, . . .

  $\frac{2}{3}$ multiples of 3 - 3, (6,) 9, 12, 15, 18, 21, 24, . . .

  6 is the lowest common multiple of 2 and 3, so it is the lowest common denominator (LCD) of $\frac{1}{2}$ and $\frac{2}{3}$.

  $$\frac{1}{2} = \frac{3}{6} \quad \text{and} \quad \frac{2}{3} = \frac{4}{6}$$

Equivalent Decimals

Decimals that name the same amount.

Example:

It helps to think of money: 30 pennies (.30) is the same amount as 3 dimes (.3).

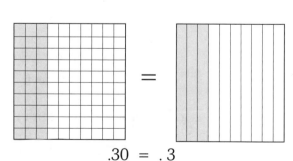

.30 = .3

Equivalent Fractions

Fractions that have the same value or name the same amount of a whole.

Example:

$\dfrac{1}{2}$

$\dfrac{2}{4}$

$\dfrac{3}{6}$

Fractions

A number that shows parts of a whole. The denominator (the number below the line) tells into how many pieces the whole has been divided. The numerator (the number above the line) indicates the number of those equal parts being considered.

Example:

$\dfrac{3}{4}$ → number of parts you have
→ number of parts into which the whole has been divided

Higher Term Fraction

A fraction is in higher terms if the numerator and the denominator have a common factor greater than 1.

Example:

Consider the fraction $\dfrac{2}{4}$

$\dfrac{2}{4}$ → factors of 2 are 1 and 2
→ factors of 4 are 1, 2, and 4
2 and 4 have 2 as a common factor.

$\dfrac{2}{4}$ is in higher terms and can be reduced by dividing the common factor, 2.

$$\frac{2}{4} = \frac{2 \div 2}{4 \div 2} = \frac{1}{2}$$

Improper Fraction

A fraction in which the numerator is greater than the denominator. Improper fractions represent values greater than one.

Example:

$$\frac{11}{3} \quad = \quad 3\frac{2}{3}$$

improper   *mixed*
fraction   *number*

Lowest Term Fraction

A fraction is in lowest terms when the numerator and the denominator have no common factors besides 1.

Example:

$$\frac{1}{3} \qquad \frac{2}{5} \qquad \frac{3}{7} \qquad \frac{11}{24}$$

Mixed Number

A number that has both a whole number part and a fractional part, such as $2\frac{1}{3}$. Mixed numbers represent values greater than 1.

Numerator

The number that is written above the line in a fraction. It tells how many parts of the whole you have or how many parts are being considered.

Example:

$$\frac{5}{8} \longleftarrow \text{ 5 is the } \textbf{numerator}$$

Percent (%)

One one-hundredth; one of one hundred parts. A fractional number with a denominator of 100. 20% means 20 out of 100.

Example:

$$5\% = \frac{5}{100} = .05 \qquad\qquad 23\% = \frac{23}{100} = .23$$

Place Value

The value given to a digit because of the place it has in the numeral. In decimal numbers, all places are fractions with denominators that are powers of ten (such as 10, 100, 1,00).

Example:

$$.5 = \frac{5}{10} \qquad\qquad .56 = \frac{56}{100}$$

$$.561 = \frac{561}{1000} \qquad\qquad .5617 = \frac{5617}{10,000}$$

Proportion

An equation that shows that two fractions are equal; written as $\frac{1}{2} = \frac{2}{4}$ or $1 : 2 :: 2 : 4$.

Ratio

A comparison of two numbers by division. It is commonly written as a fraction; however, it may be written in other ways.

$$\mathbf{\frac{3}{5}} \qquad \text{or} \qquad \mathbf{3:5} \qquad \text{or} \qquad \mathbf{3 \text{ to } 5} \qquad \text{or} \qquad \mathbf{3 \text{ of } 5}$$

Reciprocal

A number that gives a product of 1 when multiplied by the original number. To find the reciprocal of a number, exchange the denominator and the numerator.

Example:

$\frac{4}{3}$ is the reciprocal of $\frac{3}{4}$ because $\frac{4}{3} \times \frac{3}{4} = \frac{12}{12} = 1$

$\frac{1}{5}$ is the reciprocal of 5 because $\frac{1}{5} \times 5 = \frac{5}{5} = 1$

Repeating Decimal

A decimal in which one digit or a series of digits is repeated over and over again, like .3333. . . or .212121. . . Repeating decimals can be noted by using a bar over the first repeating series, like $.\overline{3}$ or $.7\overline{63}$.

Statistics and Probability

Average

A number that represents the middle or most normal of a set of numbers. Also called the mean or arithmetic mean.

- **Mean** - The sum of the collection of numbers divided by the number of numbers. To find the mean:
  - ✓ add all the numbers you have
  - ✓ divide by the number of items you added.

  Example:

  The average of 3, 9, 11, and 13 is $\dfrac{3+9+11+13}{4} = \dfrac{36}{4} = \mathbf{9}$

- **Median** -The number that would fall in the middle if the results were arranged in order from smallest to largest.

  Example:

  80 85 87 92 93   or   1 2 3 4 5 6 7 7 8 9

  median (**87**)   median (**5.5**)

- **Mode** - An average that is the number that occurs most frequently. When collecting data, you have the most of this number.

  Example:

  5, 6, 7, 7, 9, 11   **7** is the mode

Data

Facts or figures from which conclusions can be formed; information.

Extrapolate

To estimate a value beyond the known range of data by extending the known relationship or number pattern.

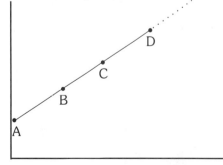

Frequency

How often something happens in a given time. The number of times an event, action, value or characteristic occurs.

Graph

A picture that shows information in an organized way. To be complete, a graph needs a title, subtitle, labeled axis, and key (when appropriate).

- **Picture Graph** - A graph that uses pictures to show quantities.

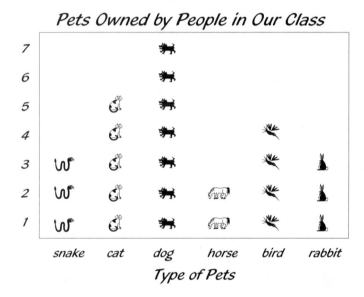

- **Bar Graph** - Graph that shows information using bars.

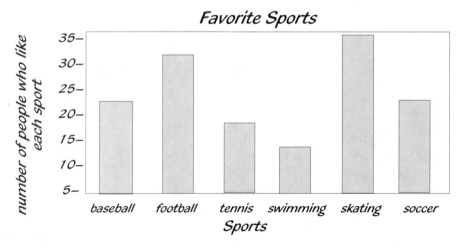

Graph, continued

- **Circle Graph** - A graph that shows all data as a percentage or a part of a circle; also called a pie graph.

Favorite Flavors of Ice Cream

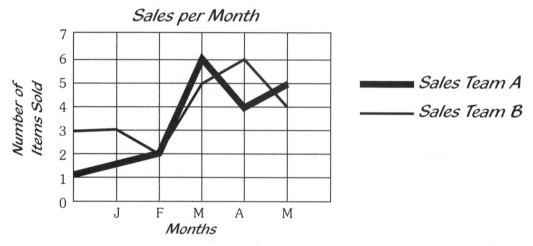

- **Line Graph** - A line graph shows information using lines. These are useful for comparing two or more things.

Sales per Month

━━━ *Sales Team A*

━━━ *Sales Team B*

- **Histogram** - A bar graph that shows how frequently data occurs. The data is usually collected in a frequency table and then put in graph form.

Ages of Students in the School

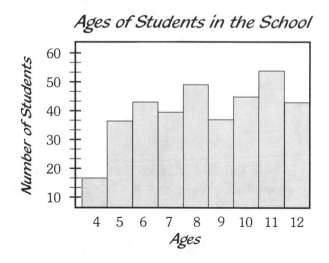

Interpolate

To find a value that is between two given values on a graph; to estimate a value between two points that are already known.

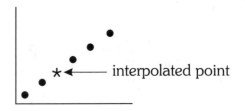

interpolated point

Mean

See Average

Median

See Average

Mode

See Average

Percent

One one-hundredth; per every hundred. A fractional number with denominator of 100.

Example:

15% means $\frac{15}{100}$ or .15

Probability

The chance that something will or will not happen.

Random

All items in the set of information or data have an equal chance of happening or not happening with a certain frequency.

Random Sample

A small portion of a larger population that is selected in such a way that all selections have an equal probability of being chosen. The sample is used as a good representation of the whole population.

Range

The difference between the smallest number and the largest number in the sample.

Example:

    $\{3, 15, 18, 27, 39\}$ range is $39 - 3 = 36$

Ratio

A comparison of two numbers by division. Ratios can be expressed several ways. The order of the in which the numbers are written is important; 1 : 4 is not the same as 4 : 1.

Example:

    A ratio can be written as **1 to 2** or **1 : 2** or $\dfrac{1}{2}$

Sample

A part taken from the whole and used to represent it.

Statistics

Numerical facts or data that can be put together or tabulated to present information about a given subject.

Stem-and-leaf Plot

A method of categorizing numerical data so that the shape of distribution can easily be seen; a way of looking at the range of data and its frequency.

Example:

ages of people in the family

11	15	23	24	29	29	31
38	38	44	47	56	57	

tens	ones
1	1 5
2	3 4 9 9
3	1 8 8
4	4 7
5	6 7

Problem Solving

Algorithm

Any special method of solving a problem.

Attribute

A characteristic, property, or quality of something; useful in classifying.

Classify

To arrange or group something into categories according to some rule or common characteristic.

Combination

Any arrangement of elements with no consideration for the order of the elements.

Example:

The combinations of the letters A, B, C, and D, taken three at a time are ABC, ABD, ACD, and BCD.

The combinations of the letters A, B, C, and D, taken two at a time are AB, AC, AD, BC, BD, and CD.

Empty Set

A set that has no elements.

Estimate

To do quick, mental calculations (often using rounding) to get an approximate answer.

Example:

$$\begin{array}{ccc}
57 & \rightarrow & 60 \\
\underline{\times 5} & & \underline{\times 5} \\
& & 300 \quad \leftarrow \text{ Answer should be about } 300
\end{array}$$

Information

- **Given Information**
  The information presented in the problem.

- **Extraneous Information**
  Information in the problem that is not necessary or relevant to solve it. Extra information.

- **Necessary Information**
  Information in the problem that must be used to solve the problem.

Intersection

A set of elements that are common to two sets, denoted by the symbol ∩.

Example:

{2, 4, 6, 8, 12} ∩ {3, 6, 9, 12, 15} = {6, 12}

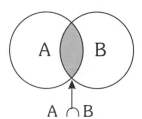

A ∩ B

Mapping

An operation that matches the members of one set with the members of another set in such a way that the pairs are uniquely paired.

Example:

Set 1		Set 2
4	→	7
7	→	10
12	→	15
22	→	25

In this relationship, 12 maps to 15 and 15 is the image of 12.

One-to-One Correspondence

A matching of *every* element in one set to a unique element in another set.

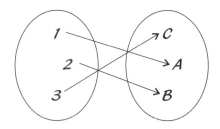

Pattern

A regular event, happening, or arrangement of numbers, objects or occurrences.

Permutation

Any of the different ordered combinations possible with a given set of elements.

Example:

The permutations of the numbers 1, 2, and 3 are
{1, 2, 3}   {1, 3, 2}   {2, 1, 3}   {2, 3, 1}   {3, 1, 2}   {3, 2, 1}

Property

A characteristic, attribute, or quality of something; useful in classifying.

Rule

A method used for solving a problem.

Set

A collection or group of numbers or other objects that follow a pattern or rule, have a common characteristic, or are the solutions to a problem.

Example:

{2, 4, 6, 8}   {10, 20, 30, 40, . . .}

{crab, lobster, shrimp, barnacle} $\{\frac{1}{2}, \frac{2}{4}, \frac{3}{6}, \frac{4}{8}, . . .\}$

Strategy

A plan of action used to solve a problem.

Subset

A set that is part of another set. It is denoted with the symbol $\subset$.

Example:

{1, 2, 3,} $\subset$ { 1, 2, 3, 4, 5}

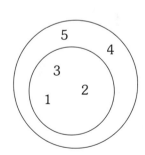

Table

A systematic arrangement of data.

Union

A set of elements that is the sum of all the elements in one set and all the elements in another set; denoted by the symbol ∪.

Example:

$\{1, 3, 5, 6\} \cup \{2, 4, 6\} = \{1, 2, 3, 4, 5, 6\}$

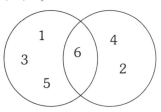

Venn Diagram

Diagrams in which intersecting circles are used to represent different sets of elements. A way to show similarities and differences; a way to compare information.

Examples:

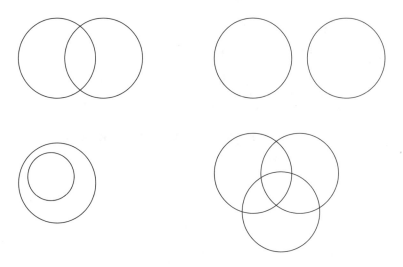

Strategies to Use to Solve Problems

✓ Use a pattern

✓ Use or make a table, chart or diagram

✓ Make an organized list

✓ Act out or use objects

✓ Guess and check

✓ Make a picture

✓ Make a simpler problem

✓ Use logical reasoning

✓ Work backwards

✓ Brainstorm for multiple answers

✓ Classify

✓ Eliminate possibilities

Steps for Successful Problem Solving

✓ **Read** the problem.

✓ **Find** the question asked or problem to be solved.

✓ **Decide** on a problem-solving strategy.

✓ **Solve**, using a problem-solving strategy.

✓ **Reread** the problem and **recheck** your work to make sure you answered the question correctly.

Examples of Operations

Division

Repeated Subtraction

$$4\,^6/_{23} \text{ or } 4 \text{ r } 6$$

```
   23)98
      -23
       75
      -23
    ⁴5¹2
      -23
       29
      -23
        6
```

✓ Subtract the divisor from the dividend.

✓ Continue to subtract the divisor until the remainder is less than the divisor.

✓ Count up the number of times that the divisor was subtracted. Write that as the quotient.

✓ Write the remainder as a remainder or as a fraction.

Use manipulatives

Use beans, counters or other objects, or draw a picture.
Count out the number of things you need to divide, or start with.
Put them equally into the number of groups you are dividing by.

Example:

$43 \div 6$

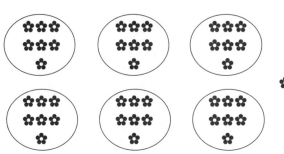

Answer: $43 \div 6 = 7$ r 1

Larger Numbers - Repeated Subtractions

1. Make a multiples table for the number you're dividing by, the divisor.
2. Subtract the largest multiple of the divisor that does not exceed the dividend.
3. When you can't subtract any more multiple of 100's, start subtracting multiples of 10's and then multiples of 1 through 9.
4. When you can't subtract any more multiples, add the number of multiples that have been subtracted. This is the quotient.

$$100 + 80 + 3 = 183$$

```
      100 + 80 + 3 = 183
  34)6243
     -3400
      2843
     -2720
       123
      -102
        21
```

Answer: **183 r 21**

Multiples Table for 34

1	34	11	374
2	68	20	680
3	102	30	1020
4	136	40	1360
5	170	50	1700
6	204	60	2040
7	238	70	2380
8	272	80	2720
9	306	90	3060
10	340	100	3400

Tiles

Count out the number of tiles you have to divide. Put them into the number of rows you are dividing by. Count the number of columns you are about to make, and then count the remainder.

Example:

$$13 \div 5$$

Answer: **2 r 3**

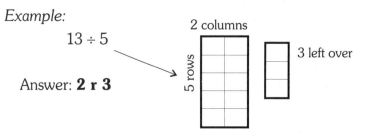

2 columns

5 rows

3 left over

Multiplication

Example:

$$4 \times 6 = 24$$

"Go by" or "Count by"

6		6
6		12
6	or	18
+6		24
24		

Draw a Picture

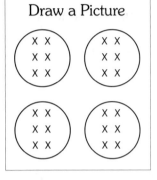

Crossed lines - count intersections

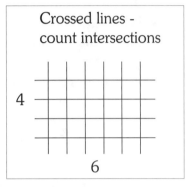

Break Aparts

$5 \times 6 =$

$3 \times 6 = 18$
$2 \times 6 = 12$

so, $18 + 12 = 30$

Break Aparts (Larger numbers)

47	40		7
x 6	x 6	+	x 6
	240	+	42

$240 + 42 = 282$

Window Pane Math $63 \times 24 = 1512$

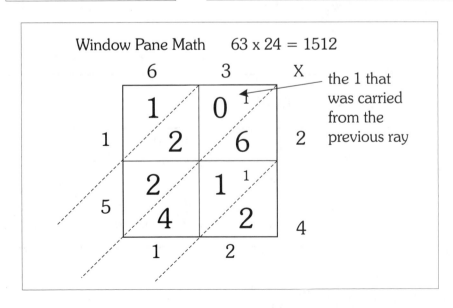

the 1 that was carried from the previous ray

63

Fractions

Finding a Common Denominator

   ✓ Multiply or divide both the numerator and denominator of a fraction by the same number.
   ✓ When fractions have a common denominator they can be compared, added and subtracted.

A common denominator for $\frac{1}{2}$ and $\frac{3}{5}$ would be 10.

$$\frac{1}{2} \times \frac{5}{5} = \frac{5}{10} \quad \text{and} \quad \frac{3}{5} \times \frac{2}{2} = \frac{6}{10}$$

Another example: A common denominator for $\frac{2}{3}$ and $\frac{1}{6}$ would be 6.

$$\frac{2}{3} \times \frac{2}{2} = \frac{4}{6} \quad \text{and} \quad \frac{1}{6} = \frac{1}{6}$$

Finding an Equivalent Fraction

   • **Method 1** - Multiply or divide by fractions equal to 1
   To find an equivalent fraction, multiply or divide both the numerator and the denominator by the same number.

$$\frac{3}{5} \times \frac{2}{2} = \frac{6}{10} \qquad \frac{16}{24} \div \frac{4}{4} = \frac{4}{6}$$

   • **Method 2** - Use multiples

$\frac{5}{8}$	multiples of 5	5	10	15	20	25	30	35
	multiples of 8	8	16	24	32	40	48	56

Fractions equivalent to $\frac{5}{8}$ are $\frac{10}{16}$, $\frac{15}{24}$, $\frac{20}{32}$, $\frac{25}{40}$, $\frac{30}{48}$, $\frac{35}{56}$, . . .

Comparing Fractions

- **Method 1** - Give the fractions a common denominator

Which is larger $\frac{3}{4}$ or $\frac{2}{3}$?

$$\frac{3}{4} \times \frac{3}{3} = \frac{9}{12} \qquad \text{and} \qquad \frac{2}{3} \times \frac{4}{4} = \frac{8}{12}$$

$\frac{9}{12}$ is larger than $\frac{8}{12}$ so $\frac{3}{4}$ is larger than $\frac{2}{3}$.

$$\frac{3}{4} > \frac{2}{3}$$

- **Method 2** - Write each fraction as a decimal and then compare the decimals.

Which is larger $\frac{5}{7}$ or $\frac{2}{3}$?

Convert $\frac{5}{7}$ to a decimal.   Convert $\frac{2}{3}$ to a decimal.

$$\frac{5}{7} = 7\overline{)5} = .71 \qquad\qquad \frac{2}{3} = 3\overline{)2} = .66$$

.71 is greater than .66   so $\frac{5}{7}$ is greater than $\frac{2}{3}$.

$$\frac{5}{7} > \frac{2}{3}$$

Converting Improper Fractions to Mixed Numbers

  ✓ Divide the numerator by the denominator.
  ✓ Write the remainder as a fraction.

$$\frac{26}{4} \qquad \rightarrow \qquad 4\overline{)26} \qquad \rightarrow \qquad 6 \text{ r } 2 \qquad \rightarrow \qquad 6\frac{2}{4}$$

Converting Mixed Numbers to Improper Fractions

✓ Multiply the denominator by the whole number.
✓ Add the numerator to the answer.
✓ Put the answer over the original denominator.

$$5\frac{3}{7} = \frac{(5 \times 7) + 3}{7} = \frac{38}{7} \quad \text{or} \quad 5\frac{3}{7} = 5\overset{+}{\underset{\times}{\nearrow}}\frac{3}{7} = \frac{(7 \times 5) + 3}{7} = \frac{38}{7}$$

$$4\frac{1}{6} = \frac{(4 \times 6) + 1}{6} = \frac{25}{6}$$

Reducing a Fraction to Lowest Terms

- **Method 1** - Use common factors
  Reducing is also called *simplifying*. To reduce (simplify) a fraction to lowest terms, find a number that can evenly divide the numerator and denominator with NO remainder. That is, find a factor of both numbers.

$$\frac{7}{14} \quad \rightarrow \quad \text{7 is a factor of both 7 and 14}$$

$$\frac{7}{14} = \frac{7 \div 7}{14 \div 7} = \frac{1}{2}$$

- **Method 2** - Use prime factorizations

  ✓ Write the prime factors of each number.

$$\frac{14}{26} \rightarrow \text{factors are } \frac{1,2,7}{1,2,13}$$

  ✓ Leave "1" alone, but cross off any other shared factors.

$$\frac{1,2,7}{1,2,13}$$

  ✓ Multiple all remaining factors.

$$\frac{1 \times 7}{1 \times 13} = \frac{7}{13}$$

  ✓ The fraction will be in lowest terms.

$$\frac{14}{26} = \frac{7}{13}$$

Adding and Subtracting Fractions

To add or subtract fractions, first look at the denominators.

- **Same Denominators**
  - ✓ Leave the denominator the same and write it in your answer.
  - ✓ Add or subtract the numerators.
  - ✓ Write the sum or difference over the denominator.
  - ✓ Simplify (reduce), if needed.

$$\frac{7}{12} + \frac{4}{12} = \frac{11}{12} \qquad \frac{3}{7} - \frac{2}{7} = \frac{1}{7} \qquad \frac{11}{12} - \frac{5}{12} = \frac{6}{12} = \frac{1}{2}$$

- **Different Denominators**
  - ✓ Find a common denominator.
  - ✓ Make equivalent fractions.
  - ✓ Add or subtract numerators.
  - ✓ Write the answer over the common denominator.
  - ✓ Reduce (simplify) if needed.

$$\begin{array}{l} \frac{2}{7} \times \frac{3}{3} = \frac{6}{21} \\ + \frac{3}{21} \qquad = \frac{3}{21} \\ \hline \qquad\qquad \frac{9}{21} = \mathbf{\frac{3}{7}} \end{array}$$

$$\begin{array}{l} \frac{1}{2} \times \frac{3}{3} = \frac{3}{6} \\ + \frac{1}{3} \times \frac{2}{2} = \frac{2}{6} \\ \hline \qquad\qquad \mathbf{\frac{5}{6}} \end{array}$$

$$\begin{array}{l} \frac{2}{3} \times \frac{5}{5} = \frac{10}{15} \\ - \frac{4}{15} \qquad = \frac{4}{15} \\ \hline \qquad\qquad \frac{6}{15} = \mathbf{\frac{2}{5}} \end{array}$$

$$\begin{array}{l} \frac{1}{2} \times \frac{5}{5} = \frac{5}{10} \\ - \frac{1}{5} \times \frac{2}{2} = \frac{2}{10} \\ \hline \qquad\qquad \mathbf{\frac{3}{10}} \end{array}$$

Finding a Decimal for a Fraction

Fractions can be represented (written) as decimals in the following way:

✓ Start with a fraction.

$$\frac{4}{8}$$

✓ Divide the numerator by the denominator.

$$8\overline{)4}$$

✓ Add a decimal point and 0's to the dividend.
Bring the decimal point straight up to the quotient.

$$8\overline{)4.00}\;^{.}$$

✓ Divide as normal.

$$\begin{array}{r} .5 \\ 8\overline{)4.0} \\ \underline{4\,0} \\ 0 \end{array}$$

✓ Write the answer with the decimal point.

$$\frac{4}{8} = .5$$

Changing a Fraction to a Percent

✓ Write the fraction as a division problem with the denominator as the divisor and the numerator as the dividend.

✓ Put a decimal point after the dividend and add zeros as needed.

✓ Complete the division problem.

✓ Multiply the answer by 100 and add a percent sign.

I have 8 out of 32. What percentage of the whole is that?

$$\frac{8}{32} \qquad \rightarrow \qquad \begin{array}{r} .25 \\ 32\overline{)8.00} \\ \underline{-\,64} \\ 160 \\ \underline{-160} \end{array} \qquad \rightarrow \qquad .25 \times 100 = \mathbf{25\%}$$

Finding a Fraction of a Number

What it means:

$\frac{3}{5}$ of 20 → break 20 into 5 groups, look at 3 of them

20

★★★★ ★★★★ ★★★★ ☆☆☆☆ ☆☆☆☆ $\frac{3}{5}$ of 20 = 12

12

- **Method 1**

To find a fraction of a number:

✓ Divide the number by the denominator.
✓ Multiply the answer by the numerator.

✓ So,

$\frac{3}{7}$ of 35

$35 \div 7 = 5$
$5 \times 3 = 15$

$\frac{3}{7}$ of 35 = 15

15 is $\frac{3}{7}$ of 35

Another Example:

$\frac{2}{9}$ of 27   → $27 \div 9 = 3$ and $3 \times 2 = 6$ →   6 is $\frac{2}{9}$ of 27

- **Method 2** (Use equivalent fractions)

$\frac{3}{7}$ of 35   = $\dfrac{3 \; (\times 5 = 15)}{7 \times 5 = 35}$

if $7 \times \mathbf{5} = 35$ then, $3 \times \mathbf{5} = 15$

therefore, $\frac{3}{7}$ of 35 = 15

Decimals

Changing a Decimal to Percent

✓ Move the decimal point two places to the right.

✓ Add a % sign.

✓ Add zeros for place holders if necessary.

.56 = 56%	.489 = 48.9%	.05 = 5%	.3 = 30%

Changing a Decimal to a Fraction

✓ Decide whether the decimal represents tenths, hundredths, thousandths, etc.

✓ Write the numerical part of the decimal over the appropriate power of 10.

✓ Reduce the fraction.

.05 is 5 hundredths

$$\frac{5}{100}$$

$$\frac{5}{100} = \frac{1}{20}$$

Comparing Decimals

This will tell you which decimal is larger or smaller. To compare decimals, you must compare the same place value.

✓ Line up the decimal points.

✓ Compare tenths, then hundredth, then thousandths.

How does 0.41 compare to 0.275?

Line up the decimal points,
$$0.41$$
$$0.275$$
↑

Look at the place values.
4 tenths (.4) is larger that 2 tenths(.2), so 0.41 is larger than 0.275
or 0.41 > 0.275

Adding Decimals

- ✓ Line up the decimal points so that the place value is in line and correct.
- ✓ Add as normal.

  hint: You can add zeros to the end of the numbers without changing the answer.

- ✓ Bring the decimal point straight down into the answer.

.75 + 2. + 1.674	3.5 + .46
.75 2.0 + 1.674 4.424	3.50 + .46 3.96

Subtracting Decimals

- ✓ Line up the decimals points so that the place value is in line.
- ✓ Subtract as normal.
- ✓ Bring the decimal point straight down into the answer.
  - ∗ Remember, you can add zeros after the decimal point in order to subtract easier.

45.9 – 2.53 →	45.90 - 2.53 43.37

Multiplying Decimals

- ✓ Solve the multiplication problem as normal.
- ✓ Count the number of places after each decimal in the problem.
- ✓ Position the decimal the same number of places in the answer.

7.56 x 1.2 1512 +7560 9.072	.56 → 2 places to the right of the decimal .2 → 1 place to the right of the decimal → 3 places to the right of the decimal in the answer

Dividing Decimals

✓ Write the problem as normal.

✓ Bring the decimal point straight up.

✓ Then divide as normal.

```
     .71
  6)4.26          4.26 ÷ 6 = 0.71
    42
    06
     6
     0
```

Percent

Changing from Percent to a Decimal

To change a percentage to a decimal, move the decimal point two places to the left. Add zeros as place holders if necessary.

56% = .56	48.9% = .489	5% = .05

Finding the Number for a Given Percent

✓ Change the percent to a decimal.

✓ Multiply the decimal times the number.

✓ Move the decimal point to the appropriate position in the answer.

What is 15% of 34?

```
      34
    x .15
     170
      34
     510
```

15% of 34 = 5.10

Finding the Percent for a Given Number

✓ Divide the number you have by the total.

✓ Change the decimal to percent.

What percent is 34 out of 50?

```
      .68
  50)34.00          .68 = 68%          34 is 68% of 50
```

Formulas

Area

square	$A = s^2$	**s** is the length of one side
rectangle	$A = l \times w$	**l** is the length, **w** is the width
triangle	$A = \frac{1}{2} b \times h$	**b** is the base, **h** is the height
parallelogram	$A = b \times h$	**b** is the base, **h** is the height
trapezoid	$A = \frac{1}{2} h (b_1 + b_2)$	**b₁** and **b₂** are the opposite, parallel sides
circle	$A = \pi r^2$	**r** is the radius

Perimeter

square	$p = 4 \times s$	**s** is the length of one side
rectangle	$p = 2 \cdot l + 2 \cdot w$	**l** is the length, **w** is the width
circle	$C = 2\pi r$	**r** is the radius
	$C = \pi d$	**d** is the diameter

Volume

cube	$V = s^3$	**s** is the length of one edge
rectangular prism	$V = l \times w \times h$	**l** is the length, **w** is the width **h** is the height
cylinder	$V = \pi r^2 h$	**r** is the radius, **h** is the height
cone	$V = \frac{1}{3} \pi r^2 h$	**r** is the radius, **h** is the height
sphere	$V = \frac{4}{3} \pi r^3$	**r** is the radius

Tables and Charts

Multiplication Chart

X	1	2	3	4	5	6	7	8	9	10	11	12
1	1	2	3	4	5	6	7	8	9	10	11	12
2	2	4	6	8	10	12	14	16	18	20	22	24
3	3	6	9	12	15	18	21	24	27	30	33	36
4	4	8	12	16	20	24	28	32	36	40	44	48
5	5	10	15	20	25	30	35	40	45	50	55	60
6	6	12	18	24	30	36	42	48	54	60	66	72
7	7	14	21	28	35	42	49	56	63	70	77	84
8	8	16	24	32	40	48	56	64	72	80	88	96
9	9	18	27	36	45	54	63	72	81	90	99	108
10	10	20	30	40	50	60	70	80	90	100	110	120
11	11	22	33	44	55	66	77	88	99	110	121	132
12	12	24	36	48	60	72	84	96	108	120	132	144

Prime Number Sieve

1	(2)	(3)	4	(5)	6	(7)	8	9	10
(11)	12	(13)	14	15	16	(17)	18	(19)	20
21	22	(23)	24	25	26	27	28	29	30
31	32	33	34	35	36	37	38	39	40
41	42	43	44	45	46	47	48	49	50
51	52	53	54	55	56	57	58	59	60
61	62	63	64	65	66	67	68	69	70
71	72	73	74	75	76	77	78	79	80
81	82	83	84	85	86	87	88	89	90
91	92	93	94	95	96	97	98	99	100

To Find Prime Numbers

✓ Cross off 1.

✓ Circle 2, 3, 5 and 7.

✓ Cross off all of the remaining multiples of 2, 3, 5, and 7.

✓ Circle the numbers that are left.

✓ The first 25 numbers have been done. Continue the procedure to find the rest of the prime numbers between 1 and 100.

Prime Factors of Numbers 2 through 100

2	prime	**27**	3^3	**52**	$2^2 \cdot 13$	**77**	$7 \cdot 11$
3	prime	**28**	$2^2 \cdot 7$	**53**	prime	**78**	$2 \cdot 3 \cdot 13$
4	2^2	**29**	prime	**54**	$2 \cdot 3^3$	**79**	prime
5	prime	**30**	$2 \cdot 3 \cdot 5$	**55**	$5 \cdot 11$	**80**	$2^4 \cdot 5$
6	$2 \cdot 3$	**31**	prime	**56**	$2^3 \cdot 7$	**81**	3^4
7	prime	**32**	2^5	**57**	$3 \cdot 19$	**82**	$2 \cdot 41$
8	2^3	**33**	$3 \cdot 11$	**58**	$2 \cdot 29$	**83**	prime
9	3^2	**34**	$2 \cdot 17$	**59**	prime	**84**	$2^2 \cdot 3 \cdot 7$
10	$2 \cdot 5$	**35**	$5 \cdot 7$	**60**	$2^2 \cdot 3 \cdot 5$	**85**	$5 \cdot 17$
11	prime	**36**	$2^2 \cdot 3^2$	**61**	prime	**86**	$2 \cdot 43$
12	$2^2 \cdot 3$	**37**	prime	**62**	$2 \cdot 31$	**87**	$3 \cdot 29$
13	prime	**38**	$2 \cdot 19$	**63**	$3^2 \cdot 7$	**88**	$2^3 \cdot 11$
14	$2 \cdot 7$	**39**	$3 \cdot 13$	**64**	2^6	**89**	prime
15	$3 \cdot 5$	**40**	$2^3 \cdot 5$	**65**	$5 \cdot 13$	**90**	$2 \cdot 3^2 \cdot 5$
16	2^4	**41**	prime	**66**	$2 \cdot 3 \cdot 11$	**91**	$7 \cdot 13$
17	prime	**42**	$2 \cdot 3 \cdot 7$	**67**	prime	**92**	$2^2 \cdot 23$
18	$2 \cdot 3^2$	**43**	prime	**68**	$2^2 \cdot 17$	**93**	$3 \cdot 31$
19	prime	**44**	$2 \cdot 11$	**69**	$3 \cdot 23$	**94**	$2 \cdot 47$
20	$2^2 \cdot 5$	**45**	$3^2 \cdot 5$	**70**	$2 \cdot 5 \cdot 7$	**95**	$5 \cdot 19$
21	$3 \cdot 7$	**46**	$2 \cdot 23$	**71**	prime	**96**	$2^5 \cdot 3$
22	$2 \cdot 11$	**47**	prime	**72**	$2^3 \cdot 3^2$	**97**	prime
23	prime	**48**	$2^4 \cdot 3$	**73**	prime	**98**	$2 \cdot 7^2$
24	$2^3 \cdot 3$	**49**	7^2	**74**	$2 \cdot 37$	**99**	$3^2 \cdot 11$
25	5^2	**50**	$2 \cdot 5^5$	**75**	$3 \cdot 5^2$	**100**	$2^2 \cdot 5^2$
26	$2 \cdot 13$	**51**	$3 \cdot 17$	**76**	$2^2 \times 19$		

Squares and Square Roots

n	n²	$\sqrt{n}$	n	n²	$\sqrt{n}$
1	1	1	26	676	5.099
2	4	1.414	27	729	5.196
3	9	1.732	28	784	5.292
4	16	2	29	841	5.385
5	25	2.236	30	900	5.477
6	36	2.45	31	961	5.568
7	49	2.646	32	1024	5.657
8	64	2.828	33	1089	5.745
9	81	3	34	1156	5.831
10	100	3.162	35	1225	5.916
11	121	3.317	36	1296	6
12	144	3.464	37	1369	6.083
13	169	3.606	38	1444	6.164
14	196	3.742	39	1521	6.245
15	225	3.873	40	1600	6.325
16	256	4.00	41	1681	6.403
17	289	4.123	42	1764	6.481
18	324	4.243	43	1849	6.557
19	361	4.359	44	1936	6.633
20	400	4.472	45	2025	6.708
21	441	4.583	46	2116	6.782
22	484	4.69	47	2209	6.856
23	529	4.796	48	2304	6.928
24	576	4.899	49	2401	7
25	625	5	50	2500	7.071

Fraction, Decimal and Percent Equivalents

Fraction	Decimal	Percent	Fraction	Decimal	Percent
$\frac{1}{25}$	.04	4%	$\frac{2}{5}$	.4	40%
$\frac{1}{20}$	.05	5%	$\frac{7}{16}$	.4375	43.75%
$\frac{1}{16}$	.0625	6.25%	$\frac{1}{2}$	.5	50%
$\frac{1}{15}$	$.0\overline{6}$	$6\frac{2}{3}$%	$\frac{9}{16}$	.5625	56.25%
$\frac{1}{12}$	$.08\overline{3}$	$8\frac{1}{3}$%	$\frac{3}{5}$	.6	60%
$\frac{1}{10}$	.1	10%	$\frac{5}{8}$	.625	62.5%
$\frac{1}{8}$	.125	12.5%	$\frac{2}{3}$	$.\overline{66}$	$66\frac{2}{3}$%
$\frac{1}{7}$	$.\overline{142857}$	$14\frac{2}{7}$%	$\frac{11}{16}$	.6875	68.75%
$\frac{1}{6}$	$.1\overline{66}$	$16\frac{2}{3}$%	$\frac{7}{10}$	.7	70%
$\frac{3}{16}$	.1875	18.75%	$\frac{3}{4}$	.75	75%
$\frac{1}{5}$	.2	20%	$\frac{4}{5}$	.8	80%
$\frac{1}{4}$	.25	25%	$\frac{13}{16}$	.8125	81.25%
$\frac{3}{10}$	.3	30%	$\frac{7}{8}$	.875	87.5%
$\frac{5}{16}$	.3125	31.25%	$\frac{9}{10}$	.9	90%
$\frac{1}{3}$	$.3\overline{33}$	$33\frac{1}{3}$%	$\frac{15}{16}$	.9375	93.75%
$\frac{3}{8}$	.375	37.5%	1	1.0	100%

Index

79